by **Jayneen Sanders**   illustrated by Dharug woman **Jasmine Seymour**

MY BODY!
What I say goes!

I0161693

Kiah's Edition

A book to empower and teach children about personal body safety, feelings, safe and unsafe touch, private parts, secrets and surprises, consent, and respectful relationships

Note to Caregivers and Educators

In this book children will learn crucial and empowering skills in personal body safety. The book can be read in one sitting but we recommend you return to each page and discuss the concepts with your child after the initial read. Discussion of the various concepts can also occur over a number of sittings. These conversations are ongoing and should happen in general daily interactions with your child. PLEASE NOTE: throughout the book we often instruct the child to tell an adult they trust (an adult on their Safety Network) if they feel unsafe. Ensure your child has three to five adults in their life who will listen to and believe them if they come with any concerns. We recommend you have a conversation with your child's chosen, trusted adults so they know how important it is to listen to and believe your child. One trusted adult should not be a family member. There are extensive Discussion Questions on pages 38-39 to further draw out the learning.

My Body! What I Say Goes! Kiah's Edition
Educate2Empower Publishing an imprint of
UpLoad Publishing Pty Ltd
Victoria Australia
www.upload.com.au

This edition first published in 2023
Text copyright © Jayneen Sanders 2023
Illustration copyright © UpLoad Publishing Pty Ltd 2023

Written by Jayneen Sanders
Illustrations by Jasmine Seymour

Jayneen Sanders asserts her right to be identified as the author of this work.
Jasmine Seymour asserts her right to be identified as the illustrator of this work.

Designed by Stephanie Spartels, Studio Spartels

ISBN: 9781761160400 (hbk) 9781761160387 (pbk)

A catalogue record for this book is available from the National Library of Australia

NATIONAL LIBRARY OF AUSTRALIA

This book was piloted by ChildSafe Australia with First Nations students and their teachers. Changes have been made to reflect their feedback. www.childsafe.org.au

ChildSafe
safe people • safe programs • safe places

Disclaimer: The information in this book is advice only written by the author based on her advocacy in this area, and her experience working with children as a classroom teacher and mother. The information is not meant to be a substitute for professional services or advice. For professional help if you are concerned about a child's behaviour, go to a health professional and/or contact the key organisations listed at www.e2epublishing.info/links

Hi! I'm Kiah. In this book you will learn how to keep your body safe, and how to say in a big, strong voice:

This is MY BODY! What I say GOES!

Feelings

Everyone has feelings.
You have feelings and I have feelings.

When I'm **happy**, I have a lovely, warm, fuzzy
feeling inside! Sometimes it makes me want to sing.
And sometimes it makes me want to dance.

WHAT DO YOU LIKE TO DO WHEN YOU FEEL HAPPY?

But sometimes I feel **sad**, and I want to cry.

You can cry when you are sad. That's why we have tears.

WHAT MAKES YOU FEEL SAD?

This child is feeling **scared**.

WHY DO YOU THINK THEY ARE FEELING SCARED?

WHAT MAKES YOU FEEL SCARED?

This child is feeling **angry**.

WHY DO YOU
THINK THEY ARE
FEELING ANGRY?

WHAT MAKES
YOU FEEL ANGRY?

This child is feeling **proud**.

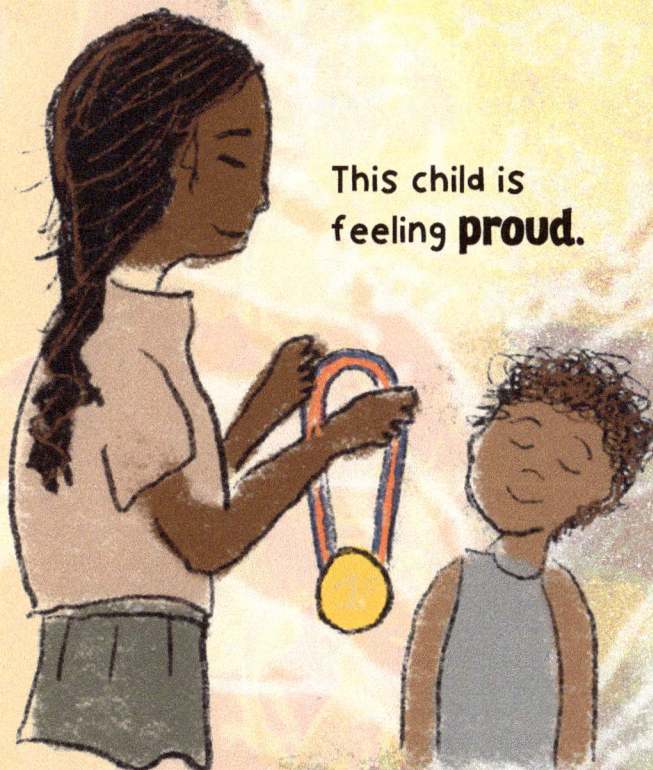

WHY DO YOU THINK
THEY ARE FEELING PROUD?

WHAT MAKES YOU
FEEL PROUD?

We all have different kinds of feelings.

SOMETIMES WE FEEL
happy
...OR
sad

...OR
ANGRY

...OR
WORRIED

...OR
SCARED.

It is important to talk about our feelings with adults we trust.

WHO CAN YOU TALK TO ABOUT YOUR FEELINGS?

WHAT DO YOU THINK 'TRUST' MEANS?

Feeling Safe

At night-time, around the campfire, I love to cuddle up with someone who makes me feel safe and who I trust. We share stories and yarn, and I snuggle in close.

I feel safe.

Some days, I love to swim in the river with my dad.

He swims beside me and holds my hand.

I feel safe.

WHEN DO YOU FEEL SAFE?

WHO MAKES YOU FEEL SAFE?

Feeling Unsafe

Sometimes I don't feel safe.

I feel **unsafe**.

I don't feel safe when Aunty Jan's dog barks at me.

I feel **unsafe**.

I don't feel safe when Kylie, from next door, pushes me down the slide.

I feel unsafe.

I don't feel safe when one of the older kids at school stands too close to me.

This makes me feel uncomfortable and **unsafe**.

When I feel unsafe or someone makes me feel uncomfortable, I know to tell an adult I trust straightaway. If they are too busy or don't believe me, then I need to tell another trusted adult.

REMEMBER!
It is never too late to tell a trusted adult what has happened and how you are feeling.

WHEN DO YOU FEEL UNSAFE?

WHO DO YOU TELL?

My Early Warning Signs

When I feel unsafe, my body lets me know. I might have a sick feeling in my tummy or my heart might beat really fast.

♥ Boom! Boom! Boom! ♥

When these things happen to my body,
I call them my Early Warning Signs.

When I feel my Early Warning Signs I know something is not right. I also know to tell an adult I trust straightaway!

HAVE YOU EVER FELT THESE EARLY WARNING SIGNS?

WHAT DID YOU DO?
WHO DID YOU TELL?

This child is feeling **unsafe.**
There are lots of Early Warning Signs
happening to this child's body.

If I feel UNSAFE my body lets me know.

SWEATY BROW

HAIR FEELS LIKE IT IS STANDING ON END

STARTS TO CRY

GOOSEBUMPS

SHAKY ALL OVER

HEART BEATS FAST

FEELS SICK IN THE TUMMY

SWEATY PALMS

NEEDS TO GO TO THE TOILET

WOBBLY LEGS

Sometimes you might feel only one or two of your Early Warning Signs and sometimes you might feel all of them.

REMEMBER!
If you feel any of your Early Warning Signs, tell an adult you trust straightaway!

CAN YOU REMEMBER SOME OF THE EARLY WARNING SIGNS?

My Safety Network

I feel safe! I have a Safety Network.

My Safety Network is made up of five adults who I trust. Anytime I feel unsafe, or I am worried or scared, I can tell one of the adults on my Safety Network. If I can't find that person, I can tell another adult on my Safety Network.

The people on my Safety Network are very important to me, and I am very important to them.

I feel SAFE! I have a Safety Network.

UNCLE JARRAH

MUM

DAD

NANA

MRS CHEN

These adults will listen to me when I tell them I feel unsafe or uncomfortable about something or someone.

Look! I have drawn around my hand. I have written the name of each adult I trust on my Safety Network hand.

My Safety Network

Uncle Jarrah

Mum

Dad

Nana

Mrs Chen

Sometimes we don't always have five adults in our lives that we can trust. If you have only three or four people on your Safety Network, that is okay too. One person should not be in your family.

My Safety Network will be different from yours.
You can choose any adults you trust and like.
You can choose an aunty, a teacher, a grandparent,
your mum or dad — anyone who makes you feel safe.
It's **your** choice!

Here is my friend Walu's Safety Network.

MUM

MRS AKEL
(NEIGHBOUR)

POP

MR BENZ
(TEACHER)

AUNTY MILLI

WHO WILL
BE ON YOUR
SAFETY NETWORK?

Private Parts
Are Private

We all have bodies. And all our bodies are different.

Some people are tall and some people are shorter. Some people have blonde hair and some people have black hair.

I have brown hair and brown eyes.

Walu has brown hair and brown eyes too.

We all have private parts. I have private parts and Walu has private parts. My private parts are those parts of my body under my bathing suit or covered by my underwear. Walu's private parts are those parts of his body under his bathing suit or covered by his underwear, too.

Everybody's mouth is a private part. Private means just for you!

People sometimes call our private parts funny names like pee pee or fanny. But we **should always** use the correct names for our private parts.

Boys usually have a penis, testicles and a bottom.

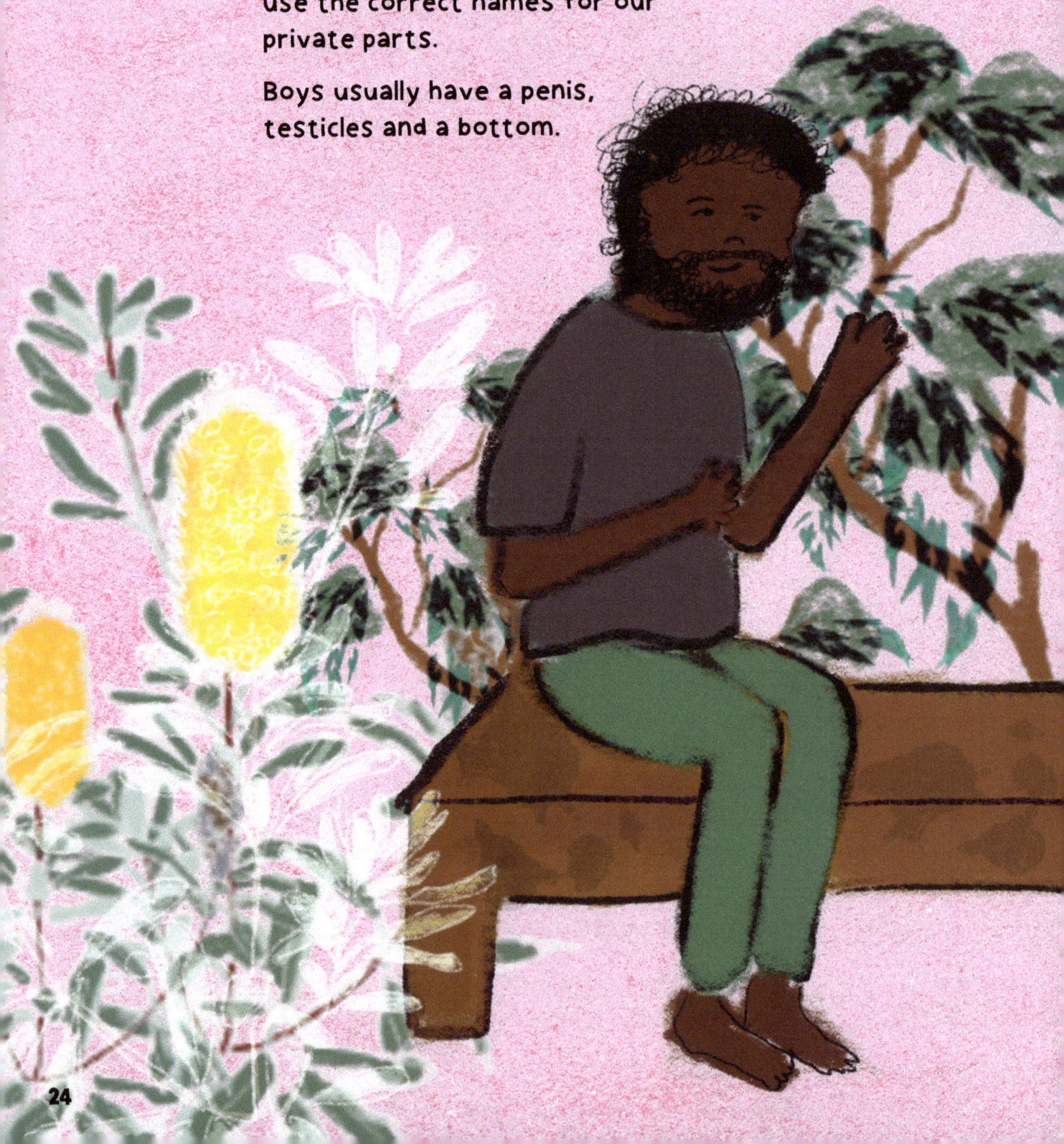

Girls usually have a vulva on the outside and a vagina on the inside. They also have nipples and a bottom. When girls get older the area around their nipples grows into breasts.

These are the **correct** names for our private parts.

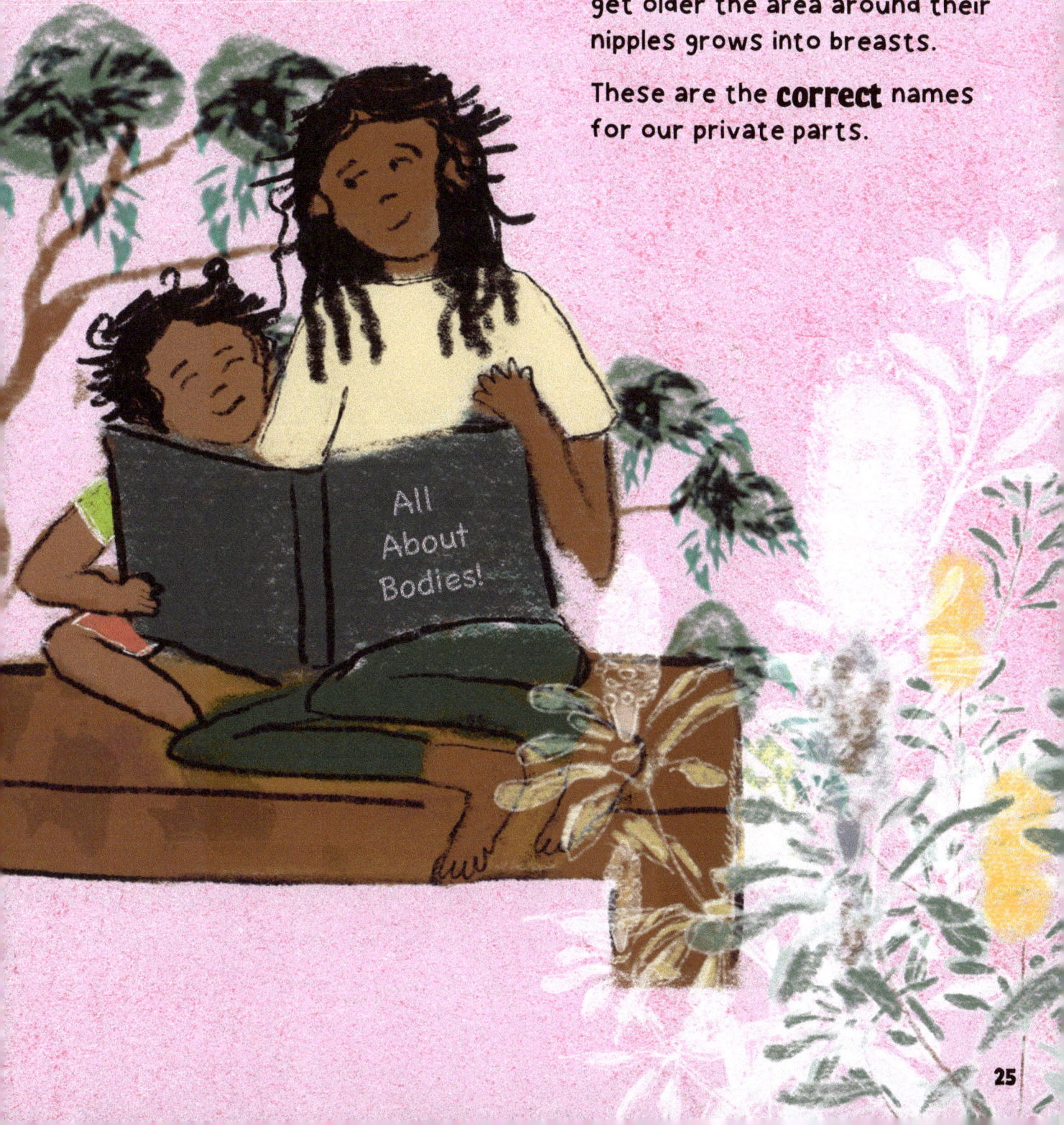

All
About
Bodies!

No-one should touch your private parts. They belong to **only** you.

When you were a baby, your parents or carer washed and dried your private parts. Now that you are older, you can wash and dry your own private parts because you are the **boss** of your body.

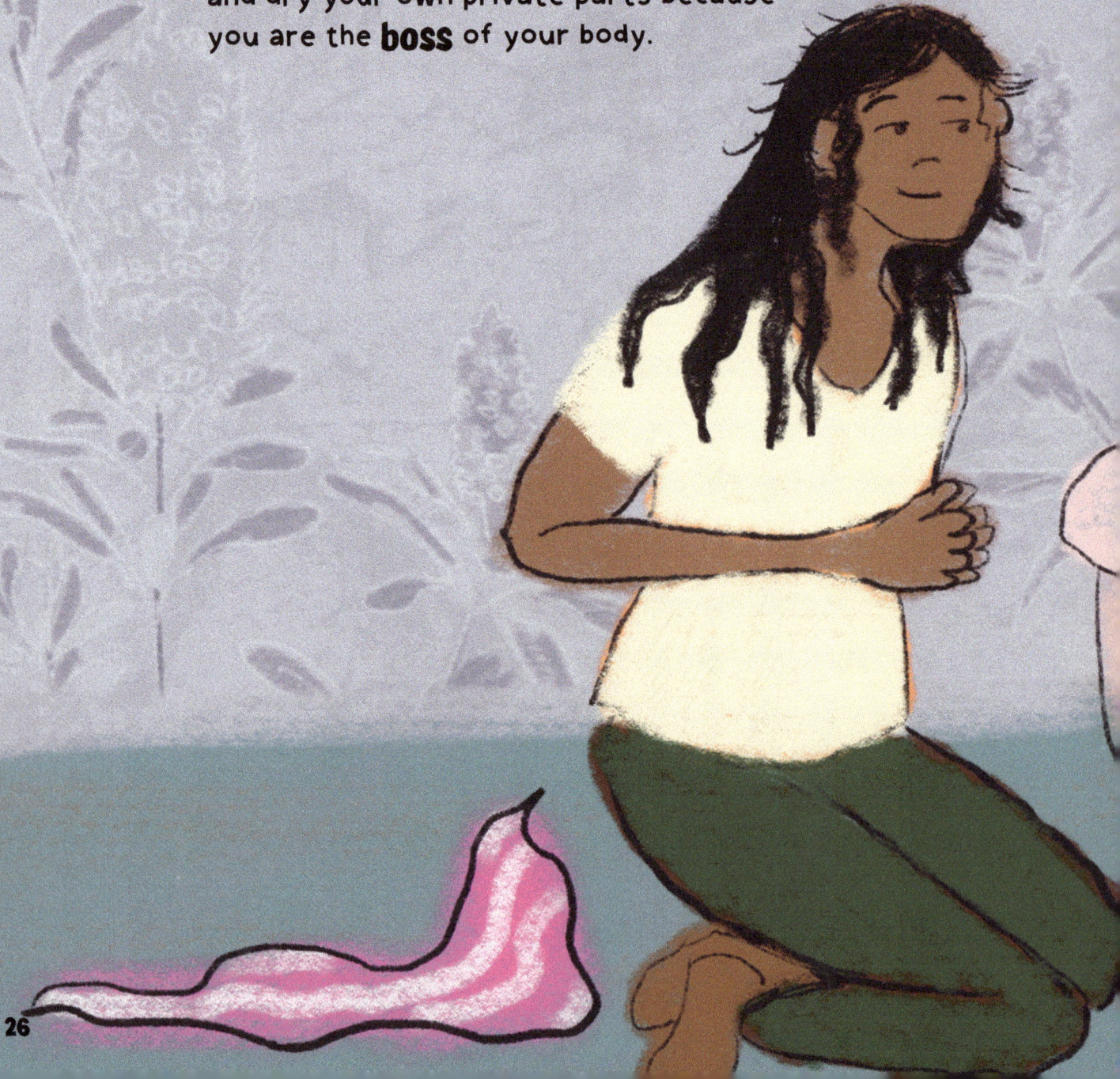

This is my body! What I say goes!

Remember!
It's **your** body!
What **you** say goes!

If someone **does** touch your private parts or wants to see your private parts you can:

1.

Say in a loud, strong voice with your hand held out, **'Stop! This is my body! What I say goes!'**

2.

Go straightaway to a trusted adult on your Safety Network and tell them exactly what happened.

If someone asks you to touch or look at their private parts or shows you pictures of private parts:

Go straightaway to a trusted adult on your Safety Network and tell them exactly what happened.

REMEMBER!
You are never ever to blame if a person acts in an unsafe way.

Sometimes if you are sick a doctor might need to check and even touch your private parts. This is only okay if an adult from your Safety Network is with you. Medical people need to ask first before they touch your body.

Secrets and Surprises

Surprises are different from secrets. Surprises are things that are happy and fun, and will **always** be told. Secrets can make you feel bad, especially if a person says you must never tell. That's why we don't have secrets in my family. We have happy surprises like not telling Pop we are coming to visit, or not telling Uncle Jarrah about his surprise birthday party.

If someone asks you to keep a secret, tell that person you don't keep secrets. You only keep happy surprises because they will be told.

I don't keep secrets!

If someone asks you to keep a secret like touching your private body parts, kissing, or showing you pictures of private parts, tell an adult on your Safety Network straightaway!

Secrets like those should be told! And even if the person tells you not to tell — secrets like those need to be told!

Hey! It's our secret! Right?

Body Boundary

We all have an invisible Body Boundary around our body.
Invisible means you can't see it ... but it's still there!

Sometimes our Body Boundary is called our **Body Bubble or Personal Space.**

People need to ask for your **consent** before giving you a kiss or a hug. Consent is special word. It means you have happily said 'Yes' to someone coming inside your body boundary. But if you don't want to kiss or hug someone, you can say, 'No, thanks', and then give them a high five or shake their hand instead. It is always your **choice**.

Remember!

It's your **body**! What you say goes!

This is MY BODY! What I say GOES!

Here are 5 BODY SAFETY RULES to remember!

1. MY BODY IS MY BODY

My body is my body and it belongs to me. I can say, 'No!' if I don't want to kiss or hug someone. I can give them a high five or shake their hand.

2. SAFETY NETWORK

I have a Safety Network. These are 3 to 5 adults who I trust. I can tell these people anything and they will believe me. If I feel worried, scared, or uncomfortable, I can tell someone on my Safety Network how I am feeling and why I feel this way.

3. EARLY WARNING SIGNS

If I feel frightened or unsafe, I might feel sick in the tummy or my heart might beat really fast. These feelings are called Early Warning Signs. If I feel this way about anything, I need to tell an adult on my Safety Network straightaway.

4. PRIVATE PARTS

I always call my private parts by their correct names. If someone asks to see or touch my private parts, or asks me to touch or look at their private parts or shows me pictures of private parts, I need to tell a trusted adult on my Safety Network straightaway.

5. NO SECRETS

I don't keep secrets, only happy surprises that will be told. If someone asks me to keep a secret, I tell them I don't keep secrets. If someone asks me to keep a secret that makes me feel unsafe or uncomfortable, I need to tell an adult on my Safety Network straightaway!

THIS IS MY BODY! WHAT I SAY GOES!

Discussion Questions
for Parents, Caregivers, and Educators

The following Discussion Questions are intended as a guide, and can be used to initiate an open and empowering dialogue with your child around personal body safety, feelings, safe and unsafe touch, private parts, secrets and surprises, consent, and respectful relationships. The questions are optional and/or can be explored at different readings. I suggest you allow your child time to answer the questions both on the internal pages and in this section, as well as, encouraging them to ask their own questions around this very important topic. It is equally important that you value their input and listen to their voice. Remain calm and confident discussing this topic with your child as they will take their cues from you. Be prepared to answer any 'challenging' questions from your child. Praise your child's responses and always reassure them of your support. These discussions will help increase your child's skills and knowledge around personal body safety, and will boost their confidence and empowerment.

Pages 4-5

Talk to you child about feeling happy. Ask, 'When do you feel happy? Do you like to dance and sing like Kiah when you are happy? What do you feel like doing when you are happy?'

Pages 6-9

Discuss various feelings such as feeling sad, scared, angry, proud, anxious or worried. Ask your child when they feel sad, scared, angry, proud, anxious or worried. For each emotion, ask, 'When you feel xxx, what do you do? Who do you talk to?' Ask, 'Why do you think it is important to talk to someone you trust about how you are feeling?'

Pages 10-11

Ask, 'When do you feel safe? Who makes you feel safe? Why? What kinds of feelings do you have inside when you feel safe?'

Pages 12-13

Ask, 'When do you feel unsafe? Does any person you know make you feel unsafe?' If your child says 'yes', ask them a bit more about that person and why they make your child feel unsafe. Ask, 'What kinds of feelings do you have inside when you feel unsafe? When you feel unsafe, who do you tell? Why do you tell that person?'

Pages 14-15

Ask, 'What is happening in this picture? How do you know Kiah is feeling her Early Warning Signs? Was Kiah right to tell an adult she trusts? How might Kiah feel if she didn't tell anyone?'

Pages 16-17

Discuss the child on page 16 and talk about their Early Warning Signs. Ask, 'When you feel unsafe, what Early Warning Signs do you get? Sometimes it is okay to feel a little bit scared, like when you go on an exciting ride at a fun park. Have you ever felt a little bit scared in an exciting way? What were you doing? How did your body tell you that you were excited, but a little bit scared? If you feel unsafe in a scared and frightened way, and your Early Warning Signs begin, what should you do straightaway? When have you felt your Early Warning Signs in an unsafe way?'

Pages 18-21

Together with your child, choose three to five adults to be on their Safety Network. Ensure one adult is not a family member. Your child will need to feel comfortable with their choices. And it is their choice, as 85% of children who reported being sexually abused knew their abuser (*NSW Commission for Children & Young People, 2009*). Your child will also need to feel comfortable that these trusted adults will always believe them if they feel worried or unsafe. Ask your child why the people they have chosen make them feel safe (be mindful of the grooming process; see the book 'Body Safety Education' for more information on grooming). The adults on your child's Safety Network should be accessible and easy for them to contact when needed. Please check in with each adult before writing their name on your child's safety hand. Make sure they know it is an honour to be chosen, how important they are to your child, and the essential role they play in your child's life. Display your child's safety hand in a prominent place. If you go to *www.e2epublishing.info* you will find a free safety hand to download, or simply trace around your child's hand. At this point, you could also share a 'safety word'. This is a word your child could say over the phone or anytime to an adult on their Safety Network, and that adult would know your child feels unsafe and the adult needs to act immediately. The word could be anything, e.g. carrots, kangaroo or dinosaur!

Pages 22-25

Discuss the word 'private' as meaning 'just for you'. Talk about private parts as those under a person's bathing suit (or underwear) and name them correctly with your child. **Note:** your child's mouth is also a private part, as are boys' nipples. Explain to your child that even though a boy's nipples are private they are not covered by a bathing suit or underwear. At this time, you may also like to introduce the word 'public'. Talk about our 'public' body parts as those that we all see such as our ears, nose and arms (but not the mouth). You could also relate 'private' and 'public' to places such as a toilet being a private place and a kitchen being a public place. Reassure your child that it is okay for them to touch their own private parts (as it can feel good) but only in a private place such as their own bedroom. If you wish to show your child appropriate drawings of private parts to discuss the difference between genders anatomically, you can download free age-appropriate line drawings of children's private parts at *www.e2epublishing.info* under Free > Teacher Downloads.

Pages 26-27

Discuss that babies and toddlers need their private parts washed by their carers but once a child is older, they can do this by themselves. Point out that your child's own trusted carer/s can dry their body but only if they feel comfortable with this, and they have asked for the child's consent.

Pages 28-29

Ask, 'What do you need to do if you are touched on your private parts?' Have your child rehearse exactly what they need to do, as on page 28. **Note:** sometimes a child may not feel confident or may be too young to say 'Stop' or 'No' as the perpetrator is someone they know well. Ensure they understand that if they don't feel confident to say 'Stop' or 'No' they should tell someone on their Safety Network straightaway. Reinforce that if they are ever touched in an unsafe way, it is never ever their fault, and it is never too late to tell a trusted adult. Discuss other situations such as a person asking your child to touch their private parts or look at images of private parts. Ask, 'What do you need to do if this happens?' Talk about how sometimes a doctor may need to touch their private parts if they are unwell, but only if an adult from their Safety Network is present. **Note:** medical professionals should always ask for a child's consent before touching any part of their body. They should always explain what they are doing and why.

Pages 30-33

Ask, 'What do you think is the difference between a surprise and a secret? What should you do if someone asks you to keep a secret? Has anyone asked you to keep a secret that made you feel bad or uncomfortable? Has anyone asked you to keep a secret that made you experience your Early Warning Signs? What did you do?' Look at the picture on page 33. Ask, 'What do you think the older boy is doing? Is Walu right to run away? How do you think he is feeling? Where do you think he is going?'

Pages 34-37

Ask, 'Do you always have to kiss or hug a person if you don't want to? Just because an adult asks you for a kiss or a hug, does that mean you have to agree? What could you do instead?' For a children's book on this topic read, 'No Means No!' available at www.e2epublishing.info Discuss how we need to ask for a person's consent if we wish to hug or kiss them, and even though parts of our bodies are 'public', it does not mean people can come inside our Body Boundary without consent. Point out that a dentist or doctor needs to ask to look in a person's mouth. Lastly, have your child stand firm, like a superhero, and say in a strong voice, 'This is MY body! What I say goes!'

Books by the Same Author

No Means No!

'No Means No!' is a children's picture book about an empowered little girl who has a very strong and clear voice in all issues, especially those relating to her body. This book teaches children about personal boundaries, respect, and consent; empowering kids by respecting their choices and their right to say, 'No!' Discussion Questions included. Suitable for children 2 to 9 years.

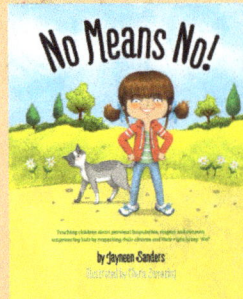

Some Secrets Should Never Be Kept

'Some Secrets Should Never Be Kept' is an award-winning and beautifully illustrated children's book that sensitively raises the subject of inappropriate touch. This book was written as a tool to help parents, caregivers, and teachers broach the subject with children in an age-appropriate and non-threatening way. Discussion Questions included. Suitable for children 3 to 11 years.

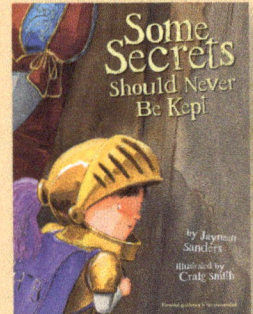

Body Safety Education
A parents' guide to protecting kids from sexual abuse

This essential and easy-to-read guide contains simple, practical, and age-appropriate ideas on how parents, carers and educators can protect children from sexual abuse — ensuring they grow up as assertive and confident teenagers and adults.

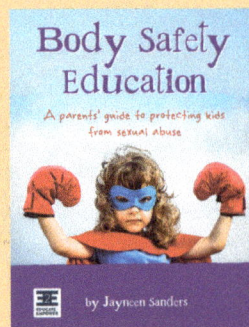

ABC of Body Safety and Consent

The 26 'key' letters and accompanying words and illustrations will help children to learn and consolidate crucial and life-changing body safety and consent skills. Discussion Questions included. Suitable for children 4 to 10 years.

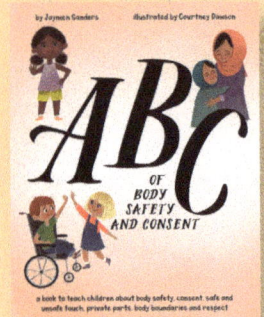

Let's Talk About Body Boundaries, Consent and Respect

Through familiar scenarios, this book opens up crucial conversations with children around consent and respect. A child growing up knowing they have a right to their own personal space, gives that child ownership and choices as to what happens to them. These concepts are presented in a child-friendly and easily-understood manner. Discussion Questions included. Suitable for children 4 to 10 years.

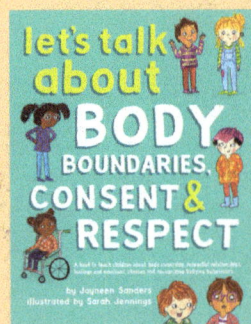

for more books and free resources go to www.e2epublishing.info

www.ingramcontent.com/pod-product-compliance
Lightning Source LLC
Chambersburg PA
CBHW041635040426
42448CB00021B/3487